Who Was
A. A. Milne?

by Sarah Fabiny

illustrated by Gregory Copeland

Penguin Workshop

For my mother,
who made sure my sisters and I visited
the Hundred Acre Wood as often as possible—SF

For Paige and Shawn—GC

PENGUIN WORKSHOP
An Imprint of Penguin Random House LLC, New York

Visit us online at www.penguinrandomhouse.com.

Library of Congress Cataloging-in-Publication Data is available upon request.

ISBN 9780451532428 (paperback)   10 9 8 7 6 5 4 3 2 1
ISBN 9780451532442 (library binding)   10 9 8 7 6 5 4 3 2 1

Contents

Who Was A. A. Milne? 1

Meet the Milnes 4

Star Student 12

Numbers or Letters? 18

Working with Words 28

War Wounds 41

A Children's Poem 55

A Book of Poems 62

A Teddy Bear and His Friends 72

Back to the Grown-Up World 84

The End of a Chapter 92

Timelines 104

Bibliography 106

Who Was A. A. Milne?

It was the end of 1925, and Christmas was just around the corner. Alan Milne's wife and son were getting ready for the holiday, but Mr. Milne was distracted. He had been asked to write a children's story for the *Evening News*, a newspaper in London, England, and he was struggling to come up with an idea. Known for writing plays and novels, he thought of himself as a "serious" writer, but he agreed to write one children's story for the Christmas edition of the paper.

His wife, Daphne, told him that it was easy—all he needed to do was write down any of the bedtime stories he told their son, Christopher Robin. Alan, who wrote under the name "A. A. Milne," was a fantastic storyteller and told his son tales of dragons, giants, and magic rings almost every night. But there was one story about a boy and his teddy bear that he thought people might find especially interesting.

So he got right to work, writing down the familiar bedtime story. He decided to name the boy in the story Christopher Robin, after his son. As for the bear, Christopher Robin had a teddy bear named Edward Bear. Could Alan use that name, also? No, it was too ordinary. He wanted the bear in his story to have a more unusual, silly, and memorable name. He named the bear Winnie-the-Pooh. And although he didn't know it yet, this bear would soon become the most famous and loved bear in children's literature.

CHAPTER 1
Meet the Milnes

Alan Milne, aged two and a half, quietly played with his toys while his older brothers, Barry and Ken, aged five and almost four, were in the middle of a reading lesson. Their father

came to check on the older boys and their studies. He pointed to a word on the blackboard in front of them and asked his sons to read it aloud. The two boys were silent—they hadn't been paying attention to the lesson. But from the corner of the room, their younger brother answered, "I can do it." Their father pointed to the word again. "Cat," Alan said. Mr. Milne smiled at his youngest son. The boy was right.

Alan Alexander Milne was born in London, England, on January 18, 1882. His mother had been a teacher, and his father ran a school for boys called Henley House. Education was an important part of the Milnes' lives—they even lived in the same building as Henley House.

John Milne was a kind and caring teacher. He wanted his students to learn as much as they could and have fun, too. Most boys started at the school when they were seven years old, including his sons Ken and Barry. But Alan was ready to start school when he was just six years old. The three brothers were all good students, but Alan was the brightest.

Alan was very excited to be at school with his brothers, especially Ken, whom he looked up to. The two were very close and did almost everything together. While their father made sure they did their schoolwork, he also encouraged them to "keep out of doors as much as you can, and see all you can of nature." And that's exactly what the brothers did. They went for long walks and bike rides, and they shared all their secrets. Sometimes they would even pretend they were the only people left on Earth and were free to do whatever they wanted. They let their imaginations run wild.

When Alan was seven years old, a new teacher came to teach science and math at Henley House. H. G. Wells would later become one of the world's most famous science-fiction writers. But at Henley House, he challenged the young boys to solve difficult math problems and research interesting science topics. He helped Alan discover a love of math.

But math wasn't the only thing Alan focused

on at Henley House. The school published a magazine, and he began writing articles for it when he was nine years old. His stories were about the things he knew best: climbing trees, chasing butterflies, running through fields, and taking long walks in the woods. Writing allowed him to use his imagination. Although he loved math, he realized he liked writing as well . . . maybe even more.

Herbert George (H. G.) Wells (1866–1946)

Herbert George (H. G.) Wells was born in Kent, England. When he was just seven years old, he had an accident that left him in bed for months. Reading became his passion. When he returned to school, he studied biology and became a science teacher. Combining his love of reading and teaching, he published his first book, *Textbook of Biology*, in 1893.

But his next book, *The Time Machine*, published in 1895, was like no other book before it. He went on to write about things that many people had never imagined: an invisible man, space travel, and aliens invading Earth. These ideas upset many people, but they made many readers think about the world in new and different ways. Some of his most important novels include *The War of the Worlds*, *The Invisible Man*, and *The First Men in the Moon*. His books were written in a genre that came to be known as science fiction.

CHAPTER 2
Star Student

Alan loved being at Henley House with Ken. It made school much more fun. But when Ken won a scholarship to go to Westminster School, he would leave his younger brother behind. Alan disliked being apart from his older brother and best friend, and he asked his parents if he could join Ken. But he was too young to go to Westminster, and his parents couldn't afford to send him there.

Alan was determined to get to Westminster, but like Ken, he would need a scholarship. He studied his hardest for the entrance exam . . . and he passed! At just eleven years old, he was the youngest student to earn a math scholarship to Westminster. It was a wonderful honor,

and he was proud to move up two grades, but
what he was most excited about was that he would
be with his brother again.

Alan brought his love of writing with him to his new school, but Westminster didn't have many classes for him to explore writing or literature, so he took to the library instead. There he read books

by Charles Dickens and Jane Austen and plays by William Shakespeare. His math scholarship got him to Westminster, but it wasn't long before he realized he'd rather spend his time writing and reading.

In 1898, it was time for Ken to graduate and begin training for a job. This was the first time the brothers would be apart. Alan would miss Ken, but they promised to write letters to each other. In their letters, they made up funny stories and rhymes. This gave Alan an idea: Their writing would be perfect for the Westminster school paper.

One day, he found a copy of the *Granta*, a magazine published by students at Cambridge University. It was a highly respected and very popular magazine that covered everything from politics to humor to literary fiction. Alan had never seen a magazine like this before, and he read it over and over again. He decided then that he would go to Cambridge and become the editor of the *Granta*. As editor, he would be in charge of the magazine. Not only would he get to choose which pieces would be published, but he would get to publish his own writing, as well. It would be the perfect first step to becoming a real writer.

Alan knew his parents couldn't afford to send him to Cambridge. However, he had set his sights on a goal, and he was determined to follow his dreams. If he had found a way to go to Westminster, he would find a way to go to Cambridge.

CHAPTER 3
Numbers or Letters?

Alan failed his first attempt at the Cambridge entrance exam. He was disappointed, but he wouldn't give up. After a second try, he passed! And in the fall of 1900, after seven years at Westminster, he made his way to Cambridge with his dream of becoming the *Granta*'s editor.

As soon as he arrived at Cambridge, he started submitting poems to the *Granta*. The same kind of silly poems he and Ken wrote together. But the editors at the magazine didn't think they were the *Granta* material and rejected them. They told Alan to keep on trying and that if he persevered, "he might one day learn to write."

He thought their comment was odd. He knew how to write, and he felt he was already a good writer! So he kept on working and submitting to the *Granta*.

Finally, one of Alan and Ken's poems was accepted, but Alan knew their work wasn't done. It would take more than just one poem to prove that he was a good writer.

As Ken and Alan grew older, they started to drift apart. Ken was too busy working to write poems with his little brother. Alan was upset,

but he wasn't going to give up on his dream of becoming editor. He would keep on writing, with or without his brother. Over the next few school terms, a steady stream of his work was published in the *Granta*. Soon, people would recognize stories and poems signed by A. A. M.—Alan Alexander Milne.

Cambridge University and *Granta*

Cambridge University, in Cambridge, England, was founded in 1209. It is the second-oldest university in the English-speaking world and the fourth-oldest university anywhere. The university is home to eight museums, a botanic garden, almost eighty sports teams, and over one hundred libraries. The libraries hold more than eight million books and journals!

Students at Cambridge founded the *Granta*

magazine in 1889. It was named after the river Cam, which runs through Cambridge. (The river was originally called the Granta.) The articles in the magazine range from humorous stories, on just about every topic, to serious articles about politics.

People all around the world now write for and read *Granta*, as it is called today.

In the spring of 1902, he received a letter from the editor of the *Granta*. He was nervous. Was this the news he was waiting for? It was! Alan was asked to take over as editor. Of course, he leaped at the chance. It was exactly why he had come to Cambridge.

His adviser warned him that he would not have time for both his studies and the magazine, but Alan was determined to prove him wrong.

Now that he was the editor, he was set on making the magazine even more well known and respected than ever. It was hard work, but he loved it. More and more people began to read the *Granta*, and its reputation grew. Alan was beginning to feel like a real writer.

During his next term at Cambridge, he received a letter from R. C. Lehmann, the founder of the *Granta*. R. C. shared that many editors and writers in London had noticed Alan's work and thought he was a talented writer. Alan couldn't believe what he was reading. Would this mean he could earn a living as a writer after Cambridge? He didn't know, but he had to find out.

Back at home, Alan's father was worried that his son was spending too much time on the magazine and not enough on his studies. He thought a career as a writer was too risky, but he saw how much it meant to his son, and he finally agreed to let him give it a try. He gave Alan £320 (about a year's salary) to help him. If the money ran out and Alan wasn't able to earn his own, he would have to give up his dream of being a writer.

Alan knew this was his one chance—and he was ready for the challenge.

CHAPTER 4
Working with Words

Alan moved to London after graduating from Cambridge, ready to take on the city as a "serious" writer. But he wasn't the only one with that dream.

He was one of many hustling to get their work published in newspapers and magazines in the big city. The competition was tough. And although some of what he wrote was published, most was rejected. By the end of his first year in London, he worried that his father might be right. Was a career as a writer too risky? He was unsure and full of doubt, but he wasn't ready to give up on his dream just yet.

Alan had a plan: If he could publish his work in *Punch*, a popular magazine that featured famous writers, it would prove that he, too, could be a real, and maybe even famous, writer. If he could get the editors of the *Granta* to publish him, he could do it with *Punch*. Finally, in May 1904, *Punch* accepted a poem from Alan titled "The New Game."

Alan's luck was beginning to change. But he still had a long journey ahead. It was the end of his first year as a writer in London, and he had spent all the money his father had given him without earning much of his own. He wanted to keep writing, but how could he afford it?

Creating stories and poems had been fun, but they didn't make him much money. Maybe Alan needed to think bigger to make it as a writer.

Punch

Henry Mayhew

Henry Mayhew and Ebenezer Landells first published *Punch* magazine on July 17, 1841. They admired other magazines published in France at the time that poked fun at the government and a traditional way of life. They wanted to bring that kind of magazine to England.

The magazine wasn't very successful at first, but it eventually became one of the most popular magazines in England. People liked the articles, but they especially liked the cartoons.

Ebenezer Landells

The magazine closed in 1992. Although it was relaunched in 1996, *Punch* closed again in 2002. Many famous authors and illustrators created work for *Punch*, including William Makepeace Thackeray, John Tenniel, and Sylvia Plath.

Maybe focusing on a book would be better for his career. So he turned to his former teacher, H. G. Wells, for advice. The famous author

encouraged Alan to give novel writing a try. And by 1905, Alan published *Lovers in London*, his first book. He had taken another big step on his path to becoming a real writer. From now on, he would devote his time to books. He was ready to move on from *Punch*, or so he thought.

He worked up the courage to tell the editor of *Punch* that he would no longer be sending in any more work. But instead of letting Alan walk away from the magazine, the editor offered him a job! The job was assistant editor, and it paid £250 a year (about $35,000 today). As an assistant editor, not only would he have a steady job and salary working at *Punch*, but his own writing would appear in the magazine every week.

Soon, people around London and all around the country were reading his work. And now that his money worries were gone, Alan was able to relax. He played tennis and went boating with friends. He was invited to fancy parties and dinners. He met important, famous people, including Winston Churchill and J. M. Barrie, the playwright of *Peter Pan*. And he would soon meet the love of his life.

Alan meets J. M. Barrie

Dorothy de Sélincourt was the goddaughter
of one of Alan's friends at *Punch*. Everyone called
her Daphne. When they met at a party in 1910,
Alan thought she "had the most perfect sense

of humor in the world." Maybe it was because she laughed at all his jokes! The two talked and laughed with each other the whole night, but they didn't see each other again until 1913.

They were both buying ski boots for separate trips when they bumped into each other. If that wasn't coincidence enough, they discovered that they were headed to the same ski resort

in Switzerland! Alan took that as a sign, and he proposed to Daphne on the ski trip. They announced their engagement as soon as they got

back to London. The two didn't know that much about each other, and their friends were surprised at how quickly the couple had gotten engaged, but they were in love.

Life was good for Alan. He was a successful writer, he had married a woman he loved very much, and the couple had just moved into a new house. With all his dreams fulfilled, he needed a new challenge. What about writing plays? Maybe Alan could add playwright to the list of things he hoped to master.

CHAPTER 5
War Wounds

But what Alan became next was a soldier. He and Daphne had only been married about a year when World War I broke out in July 1914. Alan was a pacifist, someone who believes that violence caused by war is wrong and unjust. He didn't want to join the army and fight, and at thirty-two years old, he felt he was too old to be a soldier. But many of his friends and family members signed up to join the armed forces and go off to fight. What would he do?

Eventually, he realized he would have to become a part of the war effort, so he volunteered for the army in early 1915. And he was a miserable soldier. As a successful writer, he had been in charge of his own schedule. He could do what he wanted whenever he wanted. But being in the

army meant he had to follow orders. He had to get up at a certain time, eat at a certain time, and go to bed at a certain time. He missed his freedom. Most importantly, he missed the two things he loved most: Daphne and writing. But Alan found a way to keep both in his life.

He was stationed on the Isle of Wight, an island off the southern coast of England. When Daphne visited him during his training, she wrote down all the stories he told her. Together, they realized the stories would make a good play—something interesting and exciting to help people forget about the war. They gave the play a silly, made-up title, *Wurzel-Flummery*, and sent it to playwright J. M. Barrie to read. Barrie enjoyed it very much and thought he might be able to help get it produced for the theater. Alan was excited. He could still work on becoming a playwright, even if he had to be a soldier.

But before the play could be produced, Alan was sent to France to fight in the war. His excitement soon turned to sadness and worry. His play would have to wait, he and Daphne would be apart, and maybe he wouldn't ever return home from France.

Even though Alan was against war, he fought bravely alongside his fellow soldiers. This was very tough because they fought in trenches that were muddy, cramped, smelly, and often full of rats, frogs, and lice. The disgusting conditions caused

many soldiers to get sick with a disease called
"trench fever." Alan saw soldiers killed, many of
whom were his good friends. It was a horrible
experience, and it made him hate war even more
than he had before.

World War I and Trench Warfare

World War I, or the Great War, as it was called at the time, started in 1914. Europe had split into two alliances, or sides. One alliance, called the Allied Powers, was made up of Great Britain, France, Belgium, Italy, and Russia. The other alliance, called the Central Powers, included Germany, Austria-Hungary, Bulgaria, and the Ottoman Empire (now Turkey). The Allied Powers and the Central Powers disagreed about the balance of power in Europe and about who should have the most control in the region.

Much of the fighting in World War I took place on battlefields in France. But instead of meeting on wide-open plains, soldiers fought from trenches that had been dug into the ground. These deep trenches may have helped protect them from the bullets and artillery shells they would have faced in open battlefields, but the unsanitary conditions (the damp, muddy soil) in the trenches often made soldiers very sick.

Trench warfare was not a very practical method of fighting because neither army was able to advance their position much. However, armies relied on it heavily during World War I.

In November 1916, Alan's army unit was due to launch an attack against the German army. But just before the attack, he became very ill with trench fever and could no longer fight. He was sent back to England to recover. Would this be his chance to work on *Wurzel-Flummery* again?

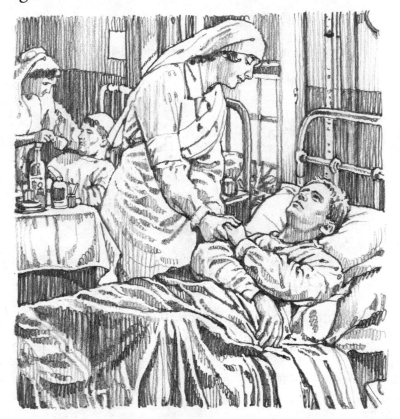

A year later, *Wurzel-Flummery* was finally produced in London, and Alan was a playwright. But this didn't mean his duties as a soldier were over. With time left to serve in the army, he needed to find a military job that he could do while he recovered from trench fever. The army recognized Alan's talent as a writer and knew they could use his help in the war office.

So Alan became a soldier by day, writing for an army unit called MI7, and a playwright by night, working on his own plays. It was tricky to balance, but his hard work paid off. Soon, many of Alan's plays were produced in London and in the United States. He was becoming well known, and some actors even asked Alan to write plays just for them!

In 1919, Alan finished serving his time in the army. Now he could focus on his writing. Later that year, Alan wrote *Mr. Pim Passes By*.

It was a play about silly misunderstandings between people. After the horror of World War I, people wanted to laugh again, and *Mr. Pim Passes By* was just what they needed to lift their spirits. It was a huge success!

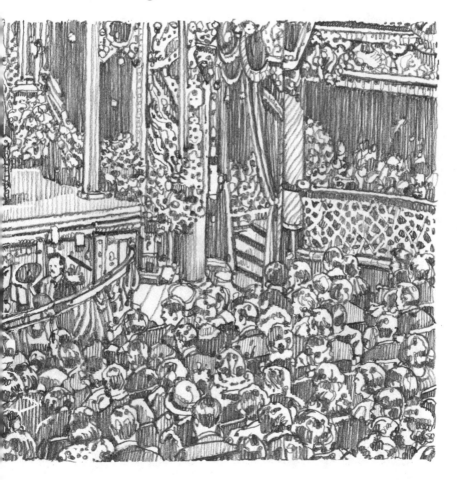

Alan and Daphne were thrilled about his successful plays, but something even more exciting was coming their way. On August 21, 1920, their son, Christopher Robin, was born. Little did Christopher Robin's parents know that one day soon their son would make his father even more famous than he already was.

CHAPTER 6
A Children's Poem

Alan couldn't believe how much his life had changed. Just a few years ago, he had been fighting in an awful war, and now he was one of the highest-paid playwrights in England and the father of a beautiful boy. Five of his plays were being performed at the same time in theaters in England and the United States. Life was good, but once again he looked for a new challenge.

He decided he would write another novel, something totally different from his last. And so he wrote a mystery novel, *The Red House Mystery*, which was published in 1922. The book

received great reviews and sold thousands of copies. Once again, he proved to himself and the world that he really was a talented author. But Alan wanted to focus on a new challenge that had nothing to do with his writing: It was time to work at becoming a great father.

One evening, Alan watched his son recite his nightly prayers before bed. This gave him an idea: He would write a poem about what he had seen.

He called the poem "Vespers" and gave it to his wife as a gift. (Evening prayer services are often called vespers.) Daphne was so impressed, she sent the poem to *Vanity Fair* magazine in New York City. And in 1923,

Vespers

Little Boy kneels at the foot of the bed,
Droops on the little hands little gold head.
Hush! Hush! Whisper who dares!
Christopher Robin is saying his prayers.

God bless Mummy. I know that's right.
Wasn't it fun in the bath tonight?
The cold's so cold, and the hot's so hot.
Oh! God bless Daddy—I quite forgot.

it was published in the January issue! "Vespers" soon became so popular that it was reprinted as a poster. People all around the world bought copies of the poster to hang on the walls of their children's bedrooms.

Later that year, the editor of a new children's magazine asked Alan to write another poem like "Vespers," but Alan wasn't interested. He felt that a "serious" and talented writer like himself wouldn't write something that was just for children.

But on a rainy vacation in Wales with his family that summer, Alan was stuck in the house, and he was bored. Since there wasn't much to do, he decided he would try to write something for the magazine editor.

He had watched Christopher Robin play with his toy soldiers, splash in puddles, and drag his teddy bear down the stairs during the vacation.

It reminded him of how he and Ken had played together when they were children, and it inspired him to write a short, silly poem called "The Dormouse and the Doctor." Alan was surprised by how quickly he was able to write it. He kept on writing. By the end of the rainy summer vacation, he had written eleven poems.

When the family returned to London, he went to see his publisher to talk about his idea for a collection of children's poems. At first, his publisher worried that it might be too big of a change for an author who had such a large adult following. But once he read Alan's poems, he saw that they were unlike anything that had been published before—they perfectly captured what it felt like to be a child. His publisher believed that both children and adults would love reading them. Now all they had to do was find the right illustrator to create drawings for the book.

His publisher suggested an illustrator named E. H. Shepard.

Alan knew about E. H. Shepard from his illustrations in *Punch* magazine, although he wasn't a fan of his work. He feared that Shepard wouldn't illustrate the characters correctly. But after seeing some sketches

E. H. Shepard

for his poem "Puppy and I," Alan knew Shepard was the perfect illustrator for his book.

CHAPTER 7
A Book of Poems

E. H. Shepard created illustrations for the poems as quickly as he could. The collection, titled *When We Were Very Young*, was published at the end of 1924. Alan and his publisher

hoped that the book would be a success, but they never could have predicted just how successful it would be. Within eight weeks, the book sold over fifty thousand copies! Bookstores ordered thousands of copies every day just to keep up with the demand. It became a best seller not only in England but also in the United States, where it was reprinted twenty-three times within the first year!

Readers, as well as critics, loved the silliness of the collection and how perfectly it captured the simple joys of childhood. The children in the poems used their imaginations, made up funny words, and played make-believe. Alan received lots of fan letters from ordinary people as well as from famous authors, movie stars, and even the president of the United States, Calvin Coolidge! He knew that his life would never be the same again.

THE WHITE HOUSE
WASHINGTON

June 6, 1924.

My Dear Mr. Milne,

I want to express my great appreciation for your wonderful stories that so vividly capture the joyful experiences of my youth in Windsor County, Vermont. Your books are a warm companion during my many travels throughout the U.S. I shall cherish your books forever.

Very truly yours,

Mr. A.A. Milne
22 Spiel Drive Cotchford Farm
Wales, England UK

In fact, life soon became extraordinarily busy. To get away from the hustle and bustle of London, Alan and Daphne bought a house in the countryside. The house was called Cotchford Farm, and it was on the edge of some woods called Ashdown Forest. Ashdown Forest had tall trees, rolling green hills, fields of flowers, and clear streams. It was the perfect place for a young boy and his stuffed animals to play.

The Milnes began spending every weekend and vacation in the countryside. Near Ashdown Forest, Christopher Robin could climb trees,

race across the fields, pick flowers, and throw sticks in the streams, just like Alan and Ken used to when they were children. Watching his son play reminded Alan of his own adventures as a boy.

But, unfortunately, Alan received some sad news about his brother soon after they bought Cotchford Farm.

Ken was sick. He had an illness called tuberculosis that was affecting his lungs. He had had to retire from his job because of his poor health and leave his home in London for Somerset, a county in southwest England. The clean air there would be better for Ken than the polluted air of London. Alan went to visit his brother when he could, but Somerset was on the other side of the country.

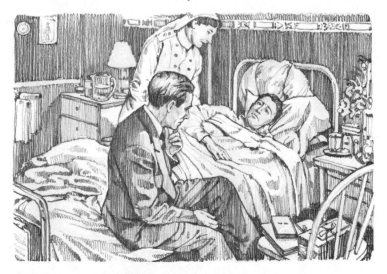

Alan was constantly worried about his brother, and soon writing became very difficult. He started on another novel but was only able to finish a few chapters. It was no use. Maybe a play would be easier for him to write? But what people really wanted was for him to create another book for children.

While he was happy that *When We Were Very Young* had been a success, he didn't want to write another children's book. He wanted to keep his reputation as a serious playwright and novelist.

Toward the end of 1925, however, the editors of the *Evening News*, a London newspaper, asked him to write just one children's story for the Christmas edition of the newspaper.

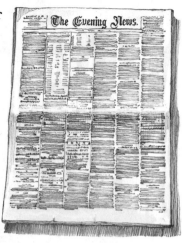

He agreed to do it, as it was just one story, but he didn't know what to write about. Daphne had an idea. She suggested that he write down one of the stories he told Christopher Robin at bedtime. Alan could manage to do that. He told Christopher Robin stories at bedtime almost every night. Some of his favorites were about a young boy and his animal friends who had adventures in the woods. So he wrote a story about Christopher Robin and his teddy bear, Winnie-the-Pooh.

How Winnie-the-Pooh Got His Name

Alan's son, Christopher Robin, was given a teddy bear on his first birthday. He called it Bear, or Teddy, or sometimes Edward Bear. But when A. A. Milne decided to include the bear in a new story, he wanted to give it a more unique name. So he searched for inspiration.

Christopher Robin loved visiting a black bear at the London Zoo named Winnie. The bear lived at the zoo from 1915 to 1934 and was one of the most popular animals there. This was a good place to start, but the name still wasn't special enough. Milne remembered the silly name of a swan his son used to feed while the family was on vacation: Pooh. And when he put the two names together, he created Winnie-the-Pooh.

CHAPTER 8
A Teddy Bear and His Friends

The story about Christopher Robin and Winnie-the-Pooh that was published in the magazine at Christmastime was a huge hit! Readers loved it, and it became even more popular than "Vespers." Its success gave Alan an idea: Maybe he should write a book of stories for

children next. Writing about Christopher Robin and Winnie-the-Pooh had been simple compared to the struggle of completing a new novel.

Alan wanted the stories to feature a whole cast of characters and knew just whom to include—Christopher Robin's other stuffed animals. The donkey, named Eeyore; the pig, named Piglet; and the mother and baby kangaroo, named Kanga and Roo, all joined Winnie-the-Pooh and Christopher Robin's adventures. Alan even decided to create two new characters, Owl and Rabbit. They all lived in a place called the Hundred Acre Wood, which felt very much like Ashdown Forest.

The Characters of Winnie-the-Pooh

A. A. Milne decided to give each of his characters a special and distinct personality, just like the members of a family.

Christopher Robin is the voice of reason. The animals look up to him and trust him to get them out of the trouble they very often get themselves into.

Winnie-the-Pooh may be "a Bear of Very Little Brain," but he is friendly, thoughtful, and a loyal friend. He's also willing to do just about anything for honey!

Piglet is small, shy, and timid. He is easily frightened, but when a situation calls for bravery, Piglet's big heart helps him overcome his fear.

Eeyore is glum, cautious, and has trouble keeping

track of his tail. He may see the worst in a situation, but he is a trustworthy friend.

Kanga is calm and patient. She also likes to have things tidy and well organized, which isn't always easy in the Hundred Acre Wood.

Roo is cheerful, energetic, and playful—and ALWAYS asking questions.

Rabbit believes he is the smartest in the group. He can be a bit bossy, but he cares a lot about his friends.

Owl sees himself as a mentor and a teacher, even if his friends don't always understand what he's talking about.

Alan wanted E. H. Shepard to illustrate the stories, and the best way for him to understand Winnie-the-Pooh was to meet him in person. So he invited the illustrator to come meet Christopher Robin and his toys at their apartment in London

and to see what their life in the country was like at Cotchford Farm. This helped E. H. Shepard imagine the world of Winnie-the-Pooh perfectly and complete the illustrations quickly.

Winnie-the-Pooh was published in October

1926 in both the United Kingdom and the United States. As expected, the book was a

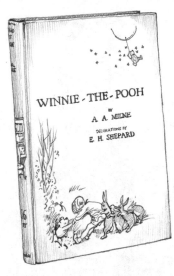

massive success! Children and adults loved it, and so did critics. The reviews said things like, "Mr. Milne has done it again," "Almost never has there been so much funniness in a book," and "Once more he has written the perfect book for children." By the end of the year, the book had sold 150,000 copies in the United States alone.

The world couldn't get enough of the stories about Christopher Robin, Winnie-the-Pooh, and all their friends. Readers loved the charming characters and the fun, silly adventures they had. Alan and his publisher were very happy with how well his children's books were selling. So even though he had never planned on writing children's books, Alan started to write even more.

He had already begun some new poems for young readers. With each poem he wrote, he remembered the writing he and Ken did together as children, and he felt inspired.

In 1927, just one year after *Winnie-the-Pooh*, his second book of poetry was published. It was called *Now We Are Six*, titled after Christopher Robin's age at the time when the poems were written. Once again, E. H. Shepard illustrated the book. Alan thought it was even better than *When We Were Very Young*.

He loved writing the poetry for *Now We Are Six*, but he knew readers were expecting new stories about the friends who lived in the Hundred Acre Wood. And so *The House at Pooh Corner* was published in 1928. In this book, Alan created new adventures for all the beloved characters

and even introduced readers to a new member of the friend family: Tigger, a very bouncy and silly tiger. Like his three other children's books, *The House at Pooh Corner* was an instant hit.

Tigger

Tigger, like most of the other characters in the Winnie-the-Pooh books, was based on one of Christopher Robin's toys—a stuffed tiger.

Tigger is full of energy and has a hard time sitting still. It's thought that his personality was based on an excitable and rowdy dog that the Milnes owned. Tigger uses his long, springy tail to bounce, and he's  very good at it. Although his bouncing does annoy his friends, sometimes.

Tigger is a confident character who knows how to have fun and be himself. He believes he's the only Tigger in the Hundred Acre Wood, and he's proud to be one of a kind!

At the end of *The House at Pooh Corner*, Alan made it clear that Christopher Robin was growing up and had to leave his friends behind. This was his way of saying he wanted to move on from children's books, and he would.

In May 1929, Alan received some terrible news. Ken, his brother and best friend, had died. He was so upset by his brother's death that he was unable to sit in the church during the funeral. Instead, he stood outside in the churchyard.

After Ken's death, he decided he would never write another children's book again. How could he write about the way Christopher Robin, Winnie-the-Pooh, and their friends played together, knowing that his memories with Ken inspired his stories? The memories of his childhood were now too painful. When Ken died, a bit of Alan's imagination died as well. There wouldn't be any more stories about the Hundred Acre Wood. Alan would go back to "serious" writing. He would focus on plays and novels.

CHAPTER 9
Back to the Grown-Up World

After Ken's death, Alan wanted to make sure that he spent time with his son, and the two became closer than ever. But while Christopher Robin was away at school, his attitude toward his father's books started to change. He didn't like the attention he got from being a character in the best-selling books. He was teased at school.

Magazines and newspapers that wanted to write articles about him wouldn't leave him alone.

People around the world wanted to know what it was like to be the son of A. A. Milne. They wanted to know what it felt like to be the famous boy who got to play in the Hundred Acre Wood. But Christopher Robin didn't want to be famous. He just wanted to be an ordinary nine-year-old boy who went to school and played with his friends.

In 1931, Alan was invited to the United States for a tour to promote his new novel, *Two People*. He received a lot of attention wherever he went, but not for being the "serious" writer he tried so hard to be. Everyone wanted to know about Christopher Robin, Winnie-the-Pooh, and the other characters in the Hundred Acre Wood. They weren't so interested in hearing about his new book for adults. This upset him very much, and he later said, "I find it's

impossible to get away from the 'Christopher Robin' atmosphere."

Christopher Robin also found it impossible to get away from the "'Christopher Robin' atmosphere." As a very young child, it had been exciting to be a character in the books and the center of attention. But as he grew older, he sometimes didn't want people to know who he was. For a while, he even dropped his middle name, Robin. Although they had been very close, Christopher Robin and his father began to grow apart.

Over the next several years, Alan wrote six more books, but only one was successful. *Peace with Honour*, published in 1934, was Alan's chance to write about his feelings on war. He believed countries and governments should avoid war at all costs and that instead, the world should strive for peace. He  felt it was the most important book he had ever written.

Five years later, World War II broke out. Great Britain, the United States, France, and the Soviet Union (the Allied Powers) were fighting Germany, Italy, and later Japan (the Axis Powers).

The war began because the leader of Germany, Adolf Hitler, wanted to expand German territory. The cruelty of Hitler and the Nazi Party in Germany shocked people around the world, including Alan. Even though *Peace with Honour* had been about the horrors of war,

World War II made Alan change his mind. He now thought that war was sometimes necessary if it meant defeating someone like Adolf Hitler.

Adolf Hitler

He began writing essays and articles urging Britain to try to win the war quickly. But he was really focused on the end of World War II because Christopher Robin had joined the British Army. He had been sent to the Middle East with the Royal Engineers.

During the war, the demand for Alan's children's books was so great that his publisher couldn't find enough paper to print them! People found comfort in the beloved characters and their peaceful lives in the Hundred Acre Wood.

The Works of A. A. Milne

A. A. Milne wrote many books, stories, and plays. Here are some of the most important ones.

- *Lovers in London*, 1905, story collection
- *Once on a Time*, 1917, novel
- *Wurzel-Flummery*, 1917, play
- *Make-Believe*, 1918, children's play
- *Mr. Pim Passes By*, 1919, play
- *The Red House Mystery*, 1922, detective novel
- *When We Were Very Young*, 1924, children's poetry collection
- *Winnie-the-Pooh*, 1926, children's story collection
- *Now We Are Six*, 1927, children's poetry collection
- *The House at Pooh Corner*, 1928, children's story collection
- *Michael and Mary*, 1930, play
- *Two People*, 1931, novel
- *Peace with Honour*, 1934, nonfiction
- *Year In, Year Out*, 1952, essay collection

CHAPTER 10
The End of a Chapter

World War II ended in 1945, and Christopher Robin returned home in 1946. Being away from his family had given him time to think. He imagined how different his life might have been if

he had not been a character in his father's books. Christopher Robin decided that he needed to keep a distance between himself and his father and, most importantly, his father's books.

Alan was hurt by his son's decision. Had he been a bad father for writing about his son? Alan saw how much comfort his books had given people during the war. Why couldn't Christopher Robin see that, too?

In 1947, Alan arranged to send the original
stuffed animals on a cross-country tour of the
United States. He asked that the toys not be
cleaned or fixed in any way. He wanted people
to see that the characters were real toys that had
been played with and loved by his son.

The tour was very successful. People traveled hundreds of miles and waited in line for hours to see Winnie-the-Pooh and his friends—well, almost all his friends. Roo was missing because Christopher Robin had lost him.

The Recent Adventures of
Winnie-the-Pooh and His Friends

Since their tour of the United States in 1947, the original stuffed animals of Winnie-the-Pooh, Piglet, Eeyore, Kanga, and Tigger have had several more adventures:

1956—Winnie-the-Pooh and his friends are put on display at E. P. Dutton & Co. Publishers (A. A. Milne's US publisher) in New York City.

1969—The friends take a trip to England for an exhibition of E. H. Shepard's drawings, in honor of his ninetieth birthday.

1976—The friends make their final visit to England to take part in Winnie-the-Pooh's fiftieth-birthday celebrations.

1987—Winnie-the-Pooh and friends are officially presented to the New York Public Library and are put on display for the public.

1988—After all the long-distance traveling, the stuffed animals are in need of a tune-up. They receive professional conservation treatment for some repairs.

1998—Winnie-the-Pooh and his friends are caught in an international argument when a British member of Parliament declares they should belong in England. The United States and England

eventually decide that the stuffed animals can call the New York Public Library their forever home.

The toys are now on permanent display at the New York Public Library.

In June 1952, Alan published his book *Year In, Year Out*, a collection of essays—some humorous and some serious, but all for adult readers. He was seventy years old at the time.

And while his plays continued to be produced, most of his other adult books were out of print. Would this be his last book?

A few months later, Alan suffered a stroke. While he rested in the hospital, Christopher Robin spoke to a newspaper reporter. He confessed that he had disliked being Christopher Robin since he was a little boy. Daphne tried to keep the interview hidden from Alan, but one of his friends told him about it during a visit. The news of his son's interview hurt Alan very much.

In December, the doctors decided that Alan would need an operation on his brain. Unfortunately, the surgery was not successful, leaving him partly paralyzed. He was unable to walk and had to use a wheelchair. He lived for another three years. During that time, he came to terms with how the world saw him. He was the author of some good plays and novels for adults, but above all, he was the creator of some of the most famous characters in children's literature.

Alan Alexander Milne, whom the world knew as A. A. Milne, died on January 31, 1956. Just after Winnie-the-Pooh was published in 1926, he had written, "I suppose that every one of us hopes secretly for immortality; to leave, I mean, a name behind him which will live forever in this world . . ." There is no doubt that A. A. Milne achieved that.

The House at Pooh Corner
Winnie-the-Pooh
The Red House Mystery
A. A. Milne
Peace With Honour

Beyond the Books

In 1930, a man named Stephen Slesinger bought the merchandising, TV, recording, and other rights to Winnie-the-Pooh from A. A Milne. That meant he was allowed to create board games, TV programs, clothing, and lots of other products that used the characters from the books. He was also responsible for adding color to the illustrations in the books. (E. H. Shepard had done the original illustrations in black and white.)

When Stephen Slesinger died, the Walt Disney Company bought the rights to the characters. They created animated versions of them, which have appeared in movies and TV programs and on everything from bedsheets and backpacks to lunchboxes and sneakers. Since then, Winnie-the-Pooh and his friends in the Hundred Acre Wood have earned more than $5.5 billion per year for the Walt Disney Company.

But Christopher Robin, Winnie-the-Pooh, Piglet, Eeyore, Kanga, Roo, Owl, Rabbit, and Tigger will always be remembered as the beloved characters created by A. A. Milne.

Timeline of A. A. Milne's Life

1882 — Alan Alexander Milne is born in London, England

1893 — Enters Westminster School

1903 — Graduates from Cambridge University

1904 — First piece published in *Punch* magazine

1906 — Goes to work at *Punch* as assistant editor

1913 — Marries Dorothy "Daphne" de Sélincourt

1916 — Sent to France to fight in World War I

1917 — First play, *Wurzel-Flummery*, is performed in London

1920 — His son, Christopher Robin, is born

— Most famous play, *Mr. Pim Passes By*, is performed in London

1923 — Writes "Vespers," first poem featuring Christopher Robin

1924 — *When We Were Very Young* is published

1926 — *Winnie-the-Pooh* is published

1927 — *Now We Are Six* is published

1928 — *The House at Pooh Corner* is published

1939 — Publishes autobiography

1952 — Suffers a stroke

1956 — Dies at the age of seventy-four on January 31

Timeline of the World

1883 — The Brooklyn Bridge opens, spanning the East River in New York City

1893 — New Zealand becomes the first country to grant women the right to vote

1900 — L. Frank Baum publishes *The Wonderful Wizard of Oz*

1914 — World War I begins with the assassination of Archduke Franz Ferdinand in Sarajevo

1919 — World War I officially ends with the signing of the Treaty of Versailles

1922 — British Egyptologist Howard Carter discovers the tomb of King Tutankhamen

1930 — Construction begins on the Empire State Building in New York City

1937 — Disney releases the animated movie *Snow White and the Seven Dwarfs*

1939 — World War II begins

1945 — World War II ends

1953 — Queen Elizabeth II is crowned queen of the United Kingdom

1957 — Russia puts the first manmade satellite, Sputnik 1, into orbit

Bibliography

*Books for young readers

Cohen, Nadia. *The Extraordinary Life of A. A. Milne*. Barnsley, England: Pen and Sword Books, 2017.

*Guillain, Charlotte. *Author Biographies: A. A. Milne*. Chicago, IL: Heinemann Library, 2012.

Kean, Danuta. "AA Milne Memoir Shows Winnie-the-Pooh Author Longing to 'Escape' His Bear." *The Guardian*, September 12, 2017. https://www.theguardian.com/books/2017/sep/12/aa-milne-memoir-shows-winnie-the-pooh-author-longing-to-escape-his-bear.

Klein, Christopher. "The True Story of the Real-Life Winnie-the-Pooh." History Stories. Last modified August 22, 2018. https://www.history.com/news/the-true-story-of-the-real-life-winnie-the-pooh.

Mass, Wendy. *History Makers: Great Authors of Children's Literature*. San Diego, CA: Lucent Books, Inc., 2000.

Miller, Mike. "Inside the True Story Behind Winnie-the-Pooh." *People*, October 13, 2017. www.people.com/movies/inside-the-true-story-behind-winnie-the-pooh.

Milne, A. A. *Autobiography*. New York: E. P. Dutton & Co., 1939.

*Milne, A. A. *The House at Pooh Corner*. New York: E. P. Dutton & Co., 1928.

*Milne, A. A. *Now We Are Six*. New York: E. P. Dutton & Co., 1927.

*Milne, A. A. *When We Were Very Young*. London: Methuen & Co., 1924.

*Milne, A. A. *Winnie-the-Pooh*. New York: E. P. Dutton & Co., 1926.

Milne, Christopher. *The Enchanted Places*. London: Pan Macmillan, 2016.

Thwaite, Ann. *A. A. Milne: The Man Behind Winnie-the-Pooh*. New York: Random House, 1990.

Thwaite, Ann. *Goodbye Christopher Robin: A. A. Milne and the Making of Winnie-the-Pooh*. New York: St. Martin's Press, 2017.

*Toby, Marlene. *A. A. Milne, Author of Winnie-the-Pooh*. A Rookie Biography. Danbury, CT: Children's Press, 1995.

*Wheeler, Jill C. *A. A. Milne*. Tribute to the Young at Heart. Edina, MN: Abdo & Daughters, 1992.

Wullschläger, Jackie. *Inventing Wonderland: The Lives and Fantasies of Lewis Carroll, Edward Lear, J. M. Barrie, Kenneth Grahame, and A. A. Milne*. New York: Free Press, 1995.